WHERE WILLIAM WALKED

Poems about Philadelphia and its people of color

VERNITA HALL

Willow Books
Detroit, Michigan

Contents

Mason-Dixon Line

The Mason-Dixon survey of 1763 mapped statehood
for Philadelphia in Pennsylvania instead of Maryland.

Where you're going depends on where you land
once lines are drawn. A free state or a slave
depends on shifting latitude   attitude
Philadelphia—a whole city changed its state

But you, couched on the corner—where will you land?
A stoned head   a headstone   a grave
state you're in   your claim on top-ography
heading south   the state where you're going

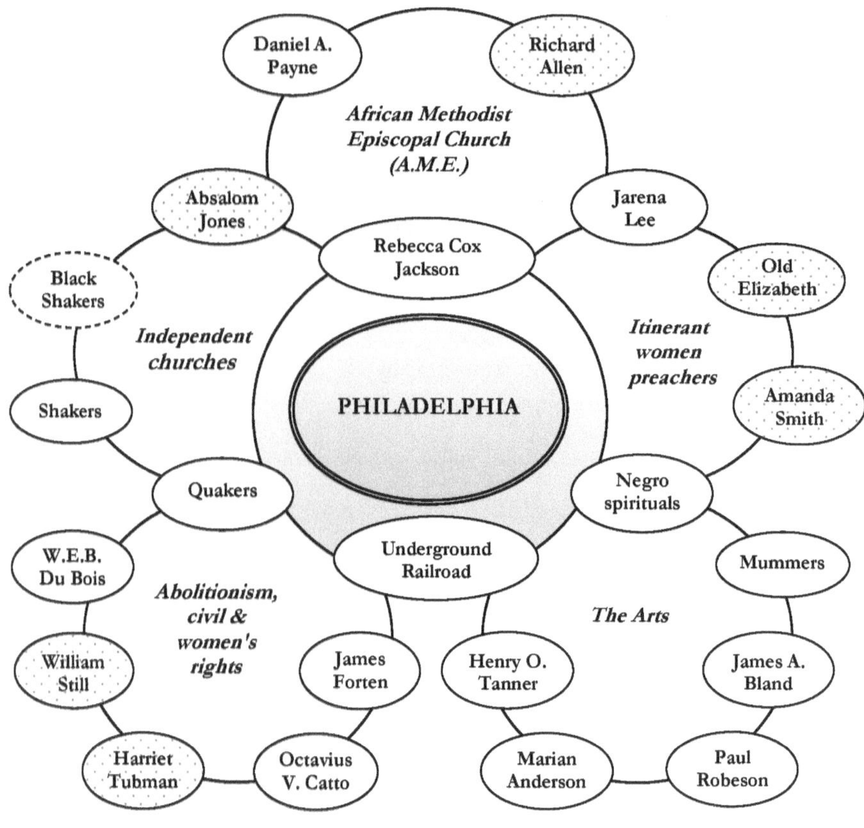

Notable African Americans with Philadelphia Connections

I. Crown of Thorns

Let your women keep silence in the churches: for it is not permitted unto them to speak…it is a shame for women to speak in the church.
— *1 Corinthians 14: 34-35*

And why should it be thought impossible, heterodox, or improper for a woman to preach? seeing the Saviour died for the woman as well as for the man.
— *Jarena Lee*

Firstborn

After a photograph of William E. B. Du Bois's son Burghardt Gomer Du Bois.
A white lace curtain partially overhangs the baby's head.

1899

My son, though Harvard-schooled, will see their blind
hatred still mock his budding brightness.
A Nigrah scholar. Thin smiles of forced politeness
will lock him tight behind the color-line.

Look, Gentle Reader: his perfect olive skin,
lithe limbs, dark curls, questing blue-brown eyes,
legs crossed to guard his manhood. For behind
his back the laced white Veil descends.

In his baby voice I heard a future prophet.
But white doctors wouldn't treat a colored child   They let—
liberty's a lie—   diphtheria fester
At eighteen months his small soul   self-sequestered

My son escaped   Not dead   not bound   He's free
Must work   Submission to such grief is slavery

A.M.E.: III. Dr. Payne Has a Dream

Submission to ignorance is slavery.
The founders of our church were unlearned men—
is this the status quo you would defend?
We need an *educated* ministry.

A man should thirst for knowledge
like a sponge hungers to drink.
He should be holy.
What he learns must be engraved
upon his heart. He must love it, live it,
then teach Bethel with a tongue
of fire and holy spirit. But
to bear the torch his lamp must first be lit!

Wilberforce could launch this dream of mine.
If you desire our equalness, train their *minds*.

Jarena's Appointment

I saw revivals among the members; though the congregation was small,
the Lord raised me up plenty of friends...for God is all in all.
— Jarena Lee

You who deny our equalness, hear my mind:

When I heard Reverend Allen preach, I said,
"This is the people to which my heart unites."
After eight years doubting, he appointed me
first female preacher of the A.M.E.
No, I never had no more than three months school.
(Lord, pardon them their errors, and make them be
careful how they handle sharp-edged tools.)

Some hearts were melted into tenderness,
but my health was broken from the constant trips.
I strove for souls, a widow's bread. Yet you
would not unite with me in fellowship.
Female preaching lacks propriety.

What obedience can cost in dignity

A.M.E.: II. Resistance

1794

Mr. C. of St. George's Church:

> Disobedience curries cost. The indignity!
> We take those Negroes in, and they presume
> parity. Cheaply preach for them—they scorn
> our charity. Thomas Jefferson
> himself remarked their lesser faculty.
> A trick of paper, they're gullible as children.

Richard Allen of Mother Bethel:

> All failed—their threats to read us out of meeting.
> But those lying elders! By God may they be damned,
> the Judas priests. They stole our church, our hope.
> A serpent coiled within their offered hand.
> Unschooled in contracts we took their help, believing
> master lynchers snaking legal rope—
>
> but two can tug.
>
>   Pray, Lord, help me forgive
> these ministers. Our new church *must* live.

Persecution by Three Ministers

But my life was hid in Christ. And in 1840, God from above spoke to him
in Albany and he troubled me no more. He had packed his trunk at night
to start for Philadelphia in the morning, and in the morning, he was dead.
    — Rebecca Cox Jackson

c. 1835

Three ministers said I ought not to live.
What death I ought to die these Methodists
appointed: stoned, or tarred and feathered, burnt,
or rolled downhill in a barrel drilled with spikes.

Good Christian men.
My principle by nature was revenge.
My strength lay in the God of power, I learnt.
Obedience would cost all that I could give.

She's chopping up the churches. She must be stopped.
Women aleading men is shameful. She
would break the marriage bed—"All lust is sin."
Their authority: they feared I meant to take
the people from their preachers, which was odd—

I had nowhere to take them, but to God

Kings Yard, Old Calabar

The moment a girl child is born, she belongs to somebody.
  — Amanda Smith, as a missionary in West Africa

1887

They've nowhere else, except to God, to run,
the trapped women I visited at King's Yard.
Four human skulls were planted in one doorway.
The sadness of their juju superstition!
Missionaries stopped that one human slaughter.

Here fathers prize their daughters—girls bring big money.
One high-toned costs a bullock (twenty dollars).
My father ransomed us from slavery—
but they still slaughter twins! The great fat queen
has slaves by the hundred. They often kill
themselves—one did. She kept his head as relic.

No Underground Railroad, Canada, nor freedom dream.
"A man's wife is his wife." None interfere, since
a female's for labor. Men have all license.

Parallel

Ashes to ashes, dust to dust;
If God won't have us, the devil must.
— from a corn-field ditty

A female can preach lay, but not be licensed.

Old Elizabeth and Amanda Smith:

I was born in Maryland. My folks were slaves
Religious people—Methodists. Sundays
Father read us from the Book of books.
Then I had a vision and got saved

Amanda: *Elizabeth:*

A great camp meeting	The brink of a fiery pit
What a revelation	Directed by the Spirit
I was told to go	Call the people to repentance
Ministers rebelled	The elders took offense
Just three months schooling	I could read but little
A colored washwoman	Dares to preach the Gospel
"Hard enough for men—	*What would women do?"*

I gave my life to service, outfoxed tricksters
high and mighty, but   those Reverend Misters

Reverend Payne Been 'Buked

But what are your reasons for refusing to have me as your pastor?
— Daniel A. Payne, at Ebenezer A.M.E. Church of Baltimore, MD

1850

Mister High-and-Mighty Doctor Payne:

The Brown Elite from Charleston is too good
to dine with common folk, or take his tea
with us, as guest. Politeness says he should.

A minister must lead through education.

Your parlor floor wears much too fine a carpet.
And women preachers?
                    Fine, for exhortation,
but not ordained or licensed for the pulpit.

Our corn-field ditties' singing you would ban.
All your learning—and you act like you're better.
We ain't all educated like yourself—
but true leaders are not always schooled in letters.

As for the "weaker sex," you priggish clubman,
see Araminta Ross—that's Harriet Tubman.

Still

*For over forty years [my] mother's heart never knew what it was to be free
from anxiety about her lost boys. But no tidings came in answer to her many
prayers, until one of them...turned up in Philadelphia. — William Still*

c. 1848

...your guide, Araminta Ross—that's Harriet Tubman.

Next customer. Sir, welcome to Philadelphia.
Peter? I'm William, the lawyer. Yes, born here.
I see you wore the yoke in Alabama

My parents bore it, too   They came from Maryland
Father bought himself   Ma twice ran clear
with her two little girls   The two sons stayed
in bondage   Forty years she's weeped and prayed

Your buried brother's name—Levin? My father's, too
You were kidnapped at six, both of you sold—when?
Your mother was Sidney?   Praise God, man   We're kin
You've found your family
                          Ma's new name is Charity

What—your wife and children, still in slavery's lurch?
Brother, for your family's freedom—let's get to work

And God Said

*But as to women preaching, he said that our Discipline knew nothing at all
about it—that it did not call for women preachers.*
    — Jarena Lee, on asking Richard Allen for permission to preach at the A.M.E.

My children, work for freedom with your brains.
Into the clay of making I unloosed
a hail of pearls in Eden, whirled a rain
of riches: first of all, the gift to *choose*.

From your rib I drew a woman-seed
and planted her to bear the fruit to come,
in equal partnership, Adam to Eve.

But ladder-huggers need a lower rung,
so men make slaves. Again. I have delivered
so many Moseses, yet you refuse
them, Pharoah-arrogant, for some are—skirted?
This Paradise I breathed is yours to lose.

There is one Master. I alone am King—
your Heavenly Father. Remember, men, My teaching.

Eulogy

"Praise the Lord!" — *Rebecca Cox Jackson, on being told of the death*
of her brother, Reverend Joseph Cox, former pastor of Bethel A.M.E.

1843

My only father, my delinquent teacher,
my sun. I fought to follow you, the preacher.
To serve my Lord as I served you, with all
my spark. You *knew* I heard the trumpet call.

They published me, and witnessed me a witch;
threatened me with stoning, as heretic;
called me "high-sensed," proud, a self-named prophet.
A word from you, my brother, could have stopped it.

I raised eight children—none of them I bore—
without complaint. Six of them were yours.
You bade me pour your coffee out
You saved me poor, then cast me out

You think that death will balm the branded hurt?
Yes, I forgive—now pour yourself   some dirt

Tablets of Moses

I could have freed a thousand more if only they knew they were slaves.
   — Harriet Tubman

Yes, I forgive. Now pour yourselves some dirt
atop that fire. Leave no sign of our camp
for trackers. Drink! (No, it will not hurt
the child—she'll sleep.) The Lord will light our lamp

there—the North Star. Here blackness is a friend,
not a stain. The Choptank River guides.
With Quakers, fearing God, we'll hide by day, then
like baby Moses, cross to freedom's side.

Turn back this train? Go on or die. My gun
will reach you 'fore the slavecatchers' horses.
I never lost a passenger—not one.
Liberty or death? Those are your choices.

I promise you a new life. You'll be *free*—
if you'll round by night, and trust this work to me.

Torn

If ever the Holy Ghost was in any place, it was in that meeting. Let her alone now.
   — A.M.E. Bishop Morris Brown, in defense of Rebecca Cox Jackson

1831

"Thee rounds one half the night, and then works hard
all day; eats nothing, till thee is worn away
to anatomy. Thee talks to nobody.
Thee don't look like thyself.

           "Good Lord, thee prays
the other half the night. I never seen
a woman like thee, wife. And now thee shuns
our marriage bed as lust. I think thee is
agoing crazy."

      "That Rebecca Jackson,
she will not join the churches. We will cut
her speaking, and her leading we will ban.
She hunts for something, but does not know what."

Go and do My work. Your God or man—
whom do you serve? Ask what you will. Oh,
your prayers are heard.

        "You ain't agoing. No."

A.M.E.: I. Exodus from St. George's

*"...and we all went out of the church in a body, and they were no more
plagued with us in the church." — Richard Allen*

Philadelphia, November 1787

Your prayers are done. You're not to sit here. No.

Trustee Jackson pointed us upstairs, so
Pa planted me an' Brother in de wayback pew.
"Pa, how come we cain't set downstairs too?"

Pa's face scrinched, like when his hand got bit
by Massa Jackson's mule, both fightin' dem plough hitches.
"Preacher Richard Allen's harvestin' too many souls,
multiplyin' 'em like loaves an' colored fishes."

"Look, Pa—dey's draggin' dat man from his knees,
from up in front. It's Reverend Absalom!
Now all our folks is leavin'. Pa? Pa! Please—"

"Son, set. You ten. A man thinks hard an' long
what he can swallow so his blood can eat. Don' cry."

But Pa sat—differently.
                                    From that day, so did I.

Crown of Thorns

A great many like to see us in the kitchen, but few in the parlor.
 — *A.M.E. Bishop William Paul Quinn*

W.E.B. Du Bois: With my Harvard education, I see how blind
submission to any man is slavery.

Jarena Lee: Do you deny our equalness? I remind
what obedience can cost in dignity.

Richard Allen: The ministers say you should heed male guidance.
You've nowhere else, except to God, to run.

Anonymous: A female's for a lay, but not a license!

Amanda Smith: Doctor Payne, might—?

Dr. Daniel Payne: You missed higher education.

William Still: Like Harriet Tubman, our resourceful leader?

Rebecca Cox Jackson: My brother gained his freedom—from my work.
My second father and reluctant teacher.
Yes, I forgave. I scrubbed his household's dirt
then rounded half the night asaving souls.

Dr. Payne: Your pleas were heard. You'll not be preachers.
No.

II. I Spoke in the Meeting

*Nine times out of ten when we look into the face of a white man
we see our enemy.*

— A.M.E. Bishop William Paul Quinn, 1852

In Pandora's Box

I.   Pandora got it wrong   the *aw-shit* moment when she jumped
onto the lid of her gift box after the plagues of man flew out
loosed by the plague of woman: curiosity   Hope doesn't
fly—that whore swims between the legs of despair and
fear   viral as saliva from a flea riding vermin bareback
craving a crevice   crack   the dark   and hides there

II. *Get in the box* she croons and she'll mount you
her photography collection of the Woodmans—
Man Ray's two moving wooden anatomically correct
in flagrante-posing figures—and she'll sign her name
on you on the recto with her nails   then she'll suck
you like a flea   III. But James Forten doesn't Gifts
his escape plan to another younger seaman (who was
probably being buggered) who climbs inside a sea
chest and hides there   Then flees the British prison
ship in a prisoner exchange   Leaves Forten to fever
and the fleas He's fifteen That itch that burning itch

IV.
Henry
Box Brown
come   inside
sings the siren
her sin-slick skin

a midnight shade
gowned in moon
beam   A brazen
Hope opens He
mails himself to
Philadelphia   but
first   he   shoves
himself into   that
narrow box and
oh good god
nails it

Shadow Man

Thomas Jefferson was a "shadow man..." — John Adams

Thomas Jefferson, you belonged in advertising:
a pitchman for tobacco, spinner of dreams,
a sculpted-prose-poseur of liberty.

Ghost writer for the Continental Congress:
when the crier read July Fourth of '76
in Philadelphia your florid creed

to four-fifths of the nation's population,
you'd missed the fine print:
                              Warning: slavery
could be hazardous to dignity.

Or did you temporize in dependence
on your colony of slaves, shackled to
a certain separate and unequal station?

Were you bound instead to your pursuit of happiness,
savoring your fine wines, your little mounts,
Monticello and mulatto Sally Hemmings?

Did you mark resemblance of her six children
to the six of your dead wife, or did you spin it,
hold this truth, too, as less self-evident?

What Goes Around

"Absconded from the household of the President of the United States,
Oney Judge..." — *The Pennsylvania Gazette*, May 24, 1796

"Absconded" my ass—Go, Oney!   Girlfriend booked it
Grabbed her getup and got the hell outta Philly
Hooked a ride on the side, kicked back with some friends
Sho' as 'kraut's cabbage, she ain't come back here again

So what if he was President   He still a skank
swapping his slaves outta state to keep from freein' 'em—
before six months, so ya couldn't call 'em "residents"
Mr. Couldn't-Tell-a-Lie jipped 'em outta their freedom

Nowadays he'd be cheatin' on his taxes
hidin' some wetbacks, payin' 'em under the table
It's always laws for they-uns and for we-uns
More brothers that got screwed large—whassup wid dat?

That high-yellow slim with freckles and nappy hair?
The Washingtons even tried twice to steal her back
Father of our country. Some father figure
When a cherry got busted, wasn't 'bout no tree—

for niggahs

The House on Third Street

September 22, 1774

No doubt they talked about the rights of man,
the rebels-in-waiting dining with Judge Ben Chew.
Glittering guests: two future Presidents,
the cream of Pensilva., the height of elegance.
John Adams penned, "The furniture was all rich."
Madeira flowed, his favorite of the wines.
George Washington sampled sweetmeats, turtle, trifles,
pitched independence from the British yoke.

Richard Allen, you'd have been fourteen then.
Had you listened at the diners' door
might all that lofty talk of liberty
have inflamed your hope for colored folk?

But not *your* eve of freedom, '74
Chew sold off your clan six years before

Soluble

When Negro Richard's family was dissolved
(sold, that is, his mother with three siblings)
grief transmuted him into a preacher
crystallized a solid purpose, kindling

another revolution. When freedom glinted
(from Master Sturgis's illiquid state)
Richard mined in haste his purchase sterling
Thus an air of hope precipitated

the hauling of salt. Once his purse was full
(eighteen months early) Richard then confounded
his former master with a gift of salt—
one bushel per saved month, whose weight rounded
would balance all his family. Only then
would he depart—as freeman Richard Allen

What compels a slave to gift his host
such ransom, then wander homeless pillar to post
for six years? His saving grace, a state of grace
that dissolved bitterness. Allen embraced
this compound: faith and forgiveness—the constitution
of a covenant sealed in a strong salt solution

My Man Richard

Trust no one till you have eaten a bushel of salt with him.
    — *German proverb*

1783

Once he got saved, my man Richard could preach
hellfire out the devil. He could teach
honest to a judge, my slave. Impossible?
Well, I've learned his word is always gospel.
He's bought his freedom papers, eighteen months early.
I never seen a Negro with his hurry.
His hands sow profit. Seems all I grow is debt.
He plants friends and faith.
                          I can't forget
I sold four of his blood. He'll probably never
see his mother again. Could you ever
forgive that act? Treat such a man as friend?

Well he served me fifteen years. Then
at our end, my slave offers a gift
to *me*, his master, Stokeley Sturgis.
Salt. He give me *eighteen bushels*. (Y'understand,
that's half a year's wages for a common man.)
In consideration of "uncommon kind
treatment of his master." And my pride?
Much it cost my manhood to accept.
Dear is freedom. Cheap goes self-respect.
For the bargain price of   humbled   I could send
my two hundred acres towards the black again.
Richard—my redeemer. Catch the irony?
My former slave—a man more free than me.

Now he's free, he took a last name—Allen.
I know he knows a name don't make a man.
We parted equals. I shook the hand—a first—
of my man—my *friend* Richard, salt of the earth.

Gift of Power

After this dream in 1831… I had a gift of power, but I knowed it not at the time.
   — *Rebecca Cox Jackson*

A Dream of Slaughter

It was 1831 when I had this dream—
I heard a footstep quick behind me. Before I could scream,
a man with a lance laid my nose open wide
He cut my head, back to front, and side to side.

He pulled my skin down, till it hung like a veil,
sliced my chest open in the form of the cross,
took my bowels out, like a butcher rids entrails.
I prayed, "Lord, receive my spirit." I feared I was lost.

After he was gone I thought to make my escape
but a voice said, "Sit still, as if you were dead."
So I stayed where I lay, though I was filled with dread.
I always had to follow what my voices said.

I was covered in blood from where the knife had sliced.
Soon the butcher came back for my heart. But then
a voice boomed out from above my head,
and God commanded him not to touch me again.

Trembling and faint, in a trouble awoken,
I cried out to my husband, "I shall die! I shall die!"
Samuel said, "What's the matter?" Then I heard these words spoken—
they were said to me thrice—"Thy life is hid in Christ."

It was the garden of the Lord, where He sowed His seed,
which is Christ in which my life is hid,
on which my life depends to be brought to the light
by the death and Resurrection of Jesus Christ.

Strengthened and humbled, I knowed in my mind
I must obey the Lord's will every day and hour.
Through these dreams and visions I would soon come to find,
though I knowed it not then, I had a gift of power.

The Death of John Cox

I had a vision of a child, floating
I saw the head and wings come through the door
Joseph asked me if I'd witnessed something
It flew upstairs, three feet from the floor
    — Rebecca Cox Jackson

1832

"John is going to die with the consumption.
He has it now." (Three days since my vision.)

"Sister, thee is going crazy. None
of our family has died from it. Son,

is thee sick?" "No, father." He was tired,
his head ached from his play. He soon retired

on his cooling board, in his ninth year.
As he wasted away, he spoke with fear

of going to Hell. He confessed to me his pile
of "awful" sins—he'd been a wicked child,

disobedient, and told lies, too.
"Why don't you pray to God, that He forgive you?"

"Lord, Thou can make me holy!" "Yes, John, He can!
Believe!" "I do! Hallelujah to the Lamb!"

"The Lord has saved my soul. Father, I
have been cured. Now I'm prepared to die."

Joseph fell, rolled on the floor, and groaned
enough to rend a heart made out of stone.

John turned his face, and looked at me and smiled.
Then he passed out of time a happy child.

I washed the clay form of the former boy
and laid him out, apraising God, with joy.

My brother may command the preacher's role,
but it was my labors saved my nephew's soul.

I am only a pen in His hand. I am just
His instrument, a worm of the dust.

Prayer of St. Harriet—Tubman

O Lord,

Convert ole mastuh. Sweeten his sour mind.
Make him a Christian (not the Southern kind).
O dear Lord, change dat man's heart, I pray—
or kill him, Lord, and take him out de way.

I Spoke in the Meeting

They don't know that I am God's bulletin board.
— Amanda Smith

I spoke in the meeting
I prayed with my sisters and cried
I spoke in the spirit
I felt the Lord's power and died

I woke in the spirit
I let it become my guide
I led in the meetings
I felt a new sense of pride

I started to question
I swam against the tide
I wouldn't be silenced
I rose up   I defied

I changed my life
I found a new way to go
I left being a wife
I learned to start saying no

All because once I—
I spoke in the meeting

Tanner's Blues

*After Henry Ossawa Tanner's Portrait of the Artist's Mother,
inspired by Whistler's Mother*

No gray and black for you—cherrywood
rippling from a walnut floor. Your gown
indigo, stroked with silver stars. A blaze, your face
aglow, a light to every room you enter
In your wake a drift of shawl, like seafoam
Your church fan charms the center

                                        I would
gift you Paris. We might stroll the Seine
at twilight, sip wine and champagne
You'd quicken there, shed this pallid languor
I could introduce you to my lions
I sketch them at the Jardin des Plantes
Cafés, music, harmony of color
everywhere

                 Come home? I'm home, at last
My color? They color me a Latin.
I'm not trying to pass. I simply—
don't announce it.
Am I a Negro? No, I—
don't renounce it

Mother, can you not try to understand?
In France I'm not a Negro—
                              I'm a man

Trans-plantation

While breeding efforts of the American Negro in captivity have been highly
successful, a failure of the species to thrive—particularly in the southern
states—has been noted

To save endangered animals from a hostile habitat, ex situ conservation has
met with limited success. That is, move some members of the population to
a new location—
Liberia, or Paris

One possible drawback, though—the original threatening ecosystem cannot
be fully re-created

Though perhaps   that's the point of the exercise

Song of the South: The Martinsville Seven, 1949

Carry me back to old Virginny,
There let me live 'till I wither and decay,
Long by the old Dismal Swamp have I wandered,
There's where this old darkey's life will pass away.
        — from the state song of Virginia (1940-1997), by James Bland

I.

Not like Rosewood, back in '23—not old Virginny
No shootin' old women, burnin' towns in old Virginny

Blacks staked four blocks in quiet East Martinsville
till the Seven were charged with rape in old Virginny

Though married, scarlet Ruby routinely thrilled,
word was, with one buck accused by old Virginny

Three fourths were high yella with good hair in Martinsville
What would they want with some ol' white trash Virginian?

But she got spied that night, as creepers will,
sharin' more than white whiskey in the backwoods of Virginia

Three boys were Hairstons—a good family name until
those Seven were fried alive by old Virginny

Dances stopped. That trucker highway finally got laid, built
on top of East Martinsville, through old Virginny

Those crackers scorched our cousins and our name. Town life stilled.
After '51 I left for Philadelphia. Bye, Virginia

Soon after, they ran Ruby out of town, the city officials
Her husband divorced her, the flower of old Virginny

I ask myself if hell takes boys who lie, what will,
Charlie, the devil make of such women from old Virginny?

II.

Six white male juries and forty-five blacks condemned brand
discrimination's stamp on old Virginny?

White rapists (though not yet) might also land
a warmed seat in the Chair of fair Virginia

Equal rights? Who fancies they command
the right to interfere with old Virginny?

Miscarried justice? We bear no double standard
We birthed this nation *here* in old Virginny

A Nigrah penned our state song—Jimmy Bland
See? Opportunity for all in old Virginny

Eminent domain. That road was *planned*
The common weal—foremost in old Virginny

Those twelve boys at UVA? The girl's OK? Understand:
Blacking their names won't fix her virginity

I ladle law in Old Dominion, pour with an even hand
Me—Governor John Battle, just a simple old Virginnyan

III.

In 1985 eleven Blacks died when Philly
bombed a bunker. (Thank God for no C-4 in old Virginny)

Forty-five minutes of burnin' killed Powelton Village
Mayor Goode claimed *Memories fade.* (Never 'bout old Virginia)

Leo Brooks testified *Never will*
this happen again, and retired to old Virginny

For me justice hangs—wherever—on one sure thing: I'm still
Charlie Green Hairston, just a Black man from Virginia

Centennial Expo, 1876

Philadelphia introduces Japanese kudzu as an ornamental plant.

Meet kudzu, the voluptuous tease
whose vine proved a killer of trees
Its immigration
unleashed an invasion
more lethal than African bees

~~~~~

The sculpture *The Death of Cleopatra* by Edmonia Lewis
was one of the most highly acclaimed exhibits.

The famed Cleopatra Edmonian
nearly died in obscurity. Wholly in
character, the queen
resurrects her routine
rigor mortis now at the Smithsonian
~~~~~

Comic-Con

After a photograph of X-men "cosplayers" (costumed players) at Philly's 2013 Comic-Con

Nowadays we celebrate imagined heroes. At Comic-Con cosplayers command
    our cred as mutants, people with X-tra ordinary powers.

Pretend again. Let's cast in capes players from history, superheroes
    of imagination and daring.

W.E.B. Du Bois as the striking Thor, god of thunder
George Washington Carver: the solitary, skinny brainiac Spiderman
Cool in the heat of righteous battle, Iceman Richard Allen
Paul Robeson, the golden—and red—Iron Man
The ultimate utility player, Octavius V. Catto—a pioneering Batman
That defiant witch-preacher Rebecca Cox Jackson as the hurricane-raising Storm
Mythic warbling warrior Marian Anderson: our Wonder Woman
Lionized of Zion, the opportunity-stalking Reverend Leon Sullivan—Black Panther
That duo of Daredevil tap dancers, the Nicholas Brothers
Speedster Dizzy Gillespie—a.k.a. The Flash—horning in
The stealthy, relentless Nightcrawler: Harriet Tubman

The KKK could play their nemesis, the Hellfire Club
And as for casting the Human Torch, that troupe has already auditioned
    any number of extras

Where William Walked

I shall throughout this study use the term "Negro," to designate all persons
of Negro descent…I shall, moreover, capitalize the word, because I believe
that eight million Americans are entitled to a capital letter.
— William Edward Burghardt Du Bois, *The Philadelphia Negro*

Philadelphia:

Where William walked the Seventh Ward to pave
    the study of *The Philadelphia Negro*.
Where Quakers walked to manumit their slaves.
Where Jimmy Bland cakewalked a minstrel show

    in *O, dem golden slippers*, before the Mummers.
Where Tanner walked in Fairmount Park to seek
    in the brush his brush with Thomas Eakins.
Where Rebecca Cox Jackson walked Negroes to join the Shakers.

Where Jarena Lee walked to plead for equal rights
    to preach—a woman—at the A.M.E.,
    where women walked in silence, out of sight.
Where Harriet walked slaves to liberty.

Where William Still and the Forten dynasty
    walked Underground to friend a freedom train.
Where Richard Allen walked away in protest,
    St. George's loss fired Mother Bethel's gain.

Where Marian meteored over Jim Crow's rails
    and Octavius Catto plucked that black bird's tail.
Where Rebecca walked tradition's nerves to read,
    twenty-two percent lack basic education.

William—first black Harvard Ph.D.
    Who follows in his steps to lead the nation
    born where William walked

Mythopoesis: The Great Seal of the United States

U.S. earthquake (Presidential resignation): August 9, 1974

I. In the Temple of Au

Once the Quaker cracked
that unfinished hump of pyramid, the eagle
soaring over the king's White House
spies movement through the break-in:

>   A partially taped mummy on a throne
>   plays with himself, tries on crowns for size:
>   the red, white, double, or the blue for war,
>   then settles on the nemes as his favorite
>   with its blue and gold stripes, its erect cobra.

>   Lounging on a divan his other favorite
>   and greatest prize: a sleek black sultry seal,
>   silky-flippered, whose cabochon ebon eyes
>   arrest him   that curvaceous spreading tail—

>   Rising, he straps on his cherished weapon:
>   the gleaming golden god flesh fashioned by
>   grieving Isis—Osiris's missing member.
>   Imagines himself now potent   or omnipotent.

But it would take the trickiness of Set
to further investigate this assignation
so the curious but too encumbered eagle
passes over that unfinished hump
with resignation

II. *Novus ordo seclorum* (The new order of the ages)

They tried to finish the unfinished pyramid
screw on the all-seeing eye   but once
it winked, the base began to churn
because a thing when screwed can turn on you

III. Judgment

In the cache-chambered pyramid whoever lies
in state—pharoah, king, or president—
lies buried here in fame or infamy
enshrined with the tailings of their office
      Wall-painted scenes of earthly life and pleasures,
      the Book of the Dead's hieroglyphic spells,
      the nemes headdress, a troop of shawbti servants,
while pitiless Anubis weighs their heart.

The just, inscribed immortal in the List
of Kings, depart to happy afterlife.
      ...birth and throne cartouches naming royalty,
          kohl-cambered eyes, face mask of gold, treasure,

Those damned descend from pillar to pillory—
eternal half-life. Shadow shrouds their Book.
      ...a slaughtered mummied bull   the flail   that crook

Brother Marinus Dreams of North Korea, Christmas 1950

Exodus   Backed against the sea
One hundred thousand panicked people   Pharoah's army
I stretch out my magic staff—   Tap the waters with my staff—   I stretch out—
Chuck that useless rod into the sea
Well, LaRue, this water-parting trick won't float
You're gonna need a boat

His crew marveled at his calm: *Captain Iron Man.*
Trusted when he volunteered their ship
to help rescue the hundred thousand jammed
onto the shell-shocked sands of Hungnam beach.
Banzai!-baying Reds surged from the north
so close they shot icicles through the heart.

The monastery's farm of Christmas trees
A mulch of needles crunches underfoot
Chirps of cricket prayer   Incense of pine flares
my nostrils and—   manure   that haunting reek
A sea of silent ghosts sprouts in the forest
Arms mushroom into branches   Reach for me

Third Infantry held "Line Charlie" under fire
while fourteen thousand piled on board—five holds
crammed like a slave ship's human cargo.
Crew of thirty-five. No translators.
Three hundred tons of jet fuel in metal drums—
and refugees lit cookfires on the lids.

The porthole of my cabin is filled with eyes
Desperation stares into my room
Suffer the little children   tapping on the window
crazed with thirst   hunger   pleading   pleading
I shutter the porthole—keep the deadlight closed
Oh Christ—for a miracle of wine   or loaves and fishes

Thirty miles of minefields to bate breath through.
No lifeboats, water, food, light, heat, toilets.
No shelter from the scything winter winds

nor respite from the putrefying stench.
A massive math of misery. But no casualties—
plus five new lives were berthed on *Meredith Victory*.

Three A.M.   I watch a spider dangling from a thread
So slim that strand   Such faith
My mind is mined with memories
Did Moses find his promised land—find peace?
I fear to sleep
I steel my deadlight closed but still—it leaks

III. The Philadelphia Story

Fight if there was a chance.

— *Octavius V. Catto*

Bop: Major League

There are people who will, if they want something, they fight, fight, fight...
and those people are very, very necessary. But there are some who hope
that, if they're doing something worthwhile, that _it_ will speak for them.
    — Marian Anderson

Octavius Valentine Catto did strike out.

That militant Mason midnight desegregated
Philly's trolleys, pitched his Pythians
into baseball's chalky color line. Manned
a brand new ballgame. But traded his first vote
for a shortstopped life (the bang bang play)

Forgotten? He swung the wide world with his hands
My Lord, what a mourning

Hushed, the throng. The Great Umpire broods god-like in his temple.
Entrails of a crow steam prophecy. Between the fluted columns
she descends, our Lady from Philadelphia. Her mink eyes close.
The perfect pitch soars.
                        And a river runs out of Eden
to undivide the light and the darkness   Crows fall
struck from the heavens like black hail   *but they never*
said a mumblin' word   not a word   not a word
And it was evening and morning   that grand-slam day

Marian's sung the wide world with her hands
Oh Lord, what a morning

Play small ball. Coach Steve says bunt, steal bases, sacrifice.
Barnstorm (summer, 2012). The Lincoln Memorial hums
with heat. Daydream....   A mob of flowers waves
bleachering the Mall's Reflecting Pool like a stadium's fans
A baseball crowds a blue curve of sky
until your mitt nets it like a butterfly

Small ball. You think: dandelions
People cross them off, too, as weeds   You see
stars, suns crowning up in vacant lots turned field
till change-up to seed head. Philly kids call 'em "Santy Clauses,"
each lacy sphere an air-flung magic lantern to rub
a wish from   Careful, girl   Catch it light, Mo'ne—eggshell-tight

—like the whole world's in your hands
My Lord, what a morning

Bringing the Heat

After Samuel Coleridge's "Kubla Khan"

August, 2014. Little League World Series.

In Williamsport
did Taneys dream of striking out
for history?

Sports-Illustrious as Octavius V.
Marian Anderson World-Serious
these South Philly sons—and Dragons' *daughter*

Her banded braids, her snake-slit eyes,
mustard pitch and firebrand's drive—
a swing and a—
                    Miss? Mo'ne! Surprise!

No little leaguers here

Weave the laurel round their heads
and cradle them in song, this team
for they have early played for stakes
and drunk the milk of victory

Marian Fever

As a girl once I swam in fever. Splashed across the ceiling, gray notes
of music pantomimed staccato. From my sickbed dimly I watched their
strobing shadow dance—cartoon hieroglyphs bounding crazily round the
border of the room, bunching blithely in the corner. A stream of quivering
quarter notes and eighths. Manic minions of delirium. Voiceless as the sea.

Years later, cruising around YouTube, I dove into Marian Anderson. Got
swallowed whole. In a high hot corner of the belly a kaleidoscope of
silvered notes thrummed, a glowing chorus pooled in concert. They waved,
bioluminescently brilliant, spinning slow in radiant unison like sardines in
a shimmering shoal. Resounding through the hollow there spewed forth
liquid sound: warble and wail, trill and tremolo. Got carried away. Bedazzled
in the monster's tumbled wake, I followed this serenest siren's song and
soaked myself in the music.

Chris Botti's "Cinema Paradiso"

The Mann Music Center, June 17, 2010

for Stephen

Tendering his lips to her mouth   round
open and inviting   stroking her
cool bronze skin   right fingers sliding
up   down   his left hand guiding   high

he lifts her   turns her   pours himself within
every hollow   Unabashed her brassy
wailing throbs the starstruck night   vibrating
their pairwise moaning sweet like violins

Turning to you as the music spelled I
spied a kindred glisten from your eyes
a wet soundless duet   our tears two half
notes thrilling toward a chord   You claimed
my hand   That's when I knew

at last   perhaps   you

That Summer, 1936

Philadelphia

Man, how they swung, after, in the Strand
Ballroom. The Freddie Fairfax Band popped it—

William "Little Oscar" Smith, sideman on bass
Dizzy's trumpet double-timing scales

Lindy Hoppers stomped their pride to stride
piano, spun ecstatic down-the-back swing-outs,

long jump turns, one sparring mob of Brown
Bombers. Ringside, upside Al Ettore

Joe Louis beat a flattening fifth-round kayo
Leaping hurdles in Berlin Jesse Owens

danced golden air steps
Everyone was on clouds

each a virtuoso torched by the jazz
that summer of high notes and heavyweights

The Boat Banger

To Marilyn Nelson, of Soul Mountain

Bosomed in her Mountain home she welcomes
all would-be rousers of some Soul-ful Muse.
A pond reflects the sumptuous house; the meadow
hums from June bugs. A drowsy peace ensues—

until the banging starts. That's how they called,
the fishermen, for help from dolphin guests
to route the tumbling schools towards the boaters,
somersaulting them into the outstretched nets.

Teacher:
Incant us inspiration—sound your drum.
Pound our boats, and bid the dolphins come.

Homographic Haiku for Sonia Sanchez

*After the "Peace is a Haiku Song" project with
the Philadelphia Mural Arts Program*

Grandmother griot—
Shout, shawoman, your peace verbs:
pacific *primers*

The Game

I have been one familiar with the game.
I have read my cards—been dealt my cards.
I have dreamed to catch Olympic flame.

I have hefted weight, trained, trained hard.
I have advanced the inching trek of pawns,
borne the scripted smiles, salved the scars.

I have dared compete before the throng—
a cheering crowd by day, a mob by night.
Swung, struck, scored, run home strong

flying the colors, infused with light
to find broken windows, the missing pet.
Burning to catch a ghost dead to rights.

You cross the line: the rules remain the same.
I have been one familiar with the game.

Robey at 12

A standout in the dugout way back when
Your face in beautiful black lights a leftist view
even then, long before you wound up
with W.E.B.

Is modesty what stretches you on the floor
horizontal, in a humble starting position,
that long wood stick angling up between your legs?
You had to be the player
The bases you stole for sport

Or, precocious stubborn maverick,
are you sitting on your anger to survive
and is its weight such you brace for
more support?

In any case, you're clearly front and centered
Those mocking, showboat eyes
among that pasty hoi polloi
staring, blazing, daring
You're the diamond

Multi-faceted, you'll shine at the triple play
Lawyer, singer, activist
No way you could ever stay small
but you won't play ball

You'll hit their pride—they'll strike back in due course
blacklist your name, bullpen your passport
Outspoken like your father you'll be
sidelined by their games, slide down
as the foul play weight of State stops you short

And as this drama plays out
Mister Twice-All-American in football at Rutgers

after your teammates have broken your bones
and you limp from the field alone

how will you bat away the rage
when they purge your glory days
from the football records page
and strike you out?

Combat

You need not always kill your enemy.
Tease the dog. Set him to chase a tail.
Bid your daughter dance him to distraction
with seven veils.

Aim modestly—just nose the race to win.
Don't charge a train head-on—loosen a rail.
Leave schemes of excess force to superpowers.
Test subtler ways.

To wound a foe removes three from the battle.
Lower his guard with flattery·and praise
and tribute—like from Greeks and snakes.
Send gifts of wooden horses and apples.

Pi Charting

Pi, the decimal, is like life—
never repeating, some say never ending

You take your measure, stumbling round, and stride,
proud and straight, the shortest path to pleasure

So sums up youth. Till fortune spirals down,
counterclockwising you. And whether then

you shortcut or wend the long way round
(although to circumnavigate is thrice

and more the length than to bisect), you're bound
from humbling to life's curves, to learn bending

Seeing Red

After the watercolor "The Old African" by Jerry Pinkney

When Jerry Pinkney painted Julius Lester's silent Old African, the one who
sought with all his magic powers to save his enslaved people, whose face did
he see?

That broad-shouldered, rippled brown back, muscular as an ocean,
wading deep into a tide of crimson, collared by a red choker necklace,
red sun streaking his skin like smeared blood.

Could be Paul Robeson.

Robey,

Did you choke up when your mother caught fire and burned? How did
you choke down the taunts when the Rutgers Scarlet Knights benched you,
because the other (Southern) team wouldn't play against a Negro?
Did you ever see red?

At Peekskill where police and the KKK found common cause, called
you "Dirty Commie" and worse, burned you in effigy, turned a joining
together in song into a bloody Pilgrims' pogrom, when civil rights went up
in smoke and the color-line bled—still no red?

Instead they claimed that you inflamed the riots. They careened your
career. You became the Red Scare poster boy, Paul Leroy, ending up
touched down at a row house in West Philly.
You might have climbed higher. Did the red backfire?

Stride into that Red Sea of hate, old African. Show your backside.
Present the other cheek to the Judas kiss. Bend this once. In the roiling
waters mark your dark reflection. In their colored scheme, whatever was
said, know this—

They never saw   red

Road Rules

I have learned
to jump-
start my car
The trick is

remembering
how you connect
cables
to leads

It's easy—
a child knows
black is always
negative

Domestic

"...a lady took me aside and said...'I know you cannot be white, but if you could be, would you not rather be white than black?'"
   — Amanda Smith

petunias   sage   green, gold-edged stalks is snake
ice-on-the-mountain   butter moistens a cake
that's chicken-in-a-basket   purple wanderin' Jew
marry you a rich white doctor   mind what I tell you

for rice puddin' and tater pies, use vanilla flavor
walnuts   peanuts   pecans   cashews my favorite
they 'bout your color   'cept your cheeks are pink as a rose
we call those tough Brazil nuts niggahtoes

no rush on children   jus' drop one or two
unless he rich   slow simmer tenders stew
keep your money in your bosom   know
your Granny loves you

fresh mint or lemon match good with a cup of tea
don't you drag home no man   as black as me

My Father's Art: Homage

*After artworks by Charles White and Henry Ossawa Tanner in the collection
of Bill and Camille Cosby*

"He was my hero." — Bill Cosby, speaking of murdered son Ennis

All my life that was, that glowering face,
eyes rife with accusation, question marks
as brows, silent censure from the dead
serious folded tuck of arms, your billboard-
sized shadow—Mother's showpiece:
the looming charcoal sketch starring

Our-Father-which-art-holier-than-thou. Bill,
the artist named it. As if daily facing
one such scowl were insufficient showing.
But Homage to Langston Hughes? Remarkable
how its mirrored stance of you became my polestar.
Me, The Problem, the dyslexic deadbeat

third note of your blood arpeggio, dead
last of all your trophies. What if your star
had fallen back to the Richard Allen projects, and bills
posed us among The Thankful Poor? Face
that, or this: cast me again a mark
with a flat   at night   alone   in that showy

Mercedes. Would we still choose the latter show
for a lifetime of these residuals, I wonder? [Dead
silence] You bet your life. Dad, my time was marked.
And I would not trade all of heaven's stars
for what you've earned. But having to face
the loss of your only son was—overbilling.

To tell the truth, I enjoyed being billed
the rebel. A prince is due some showboating
after all. Funny, though, how façades
loosen with age, slough off like dead
skin. Now I can see our family in the starburst
behind that youth, his scowl like a birthmark

I inherited. The white bird's billowing
wings, gentle as Mother's. The stand-up showman's
charcoal ticker tape of minstrel faces.
For each of my sisters' dreams: four blue stars.
All my father's art. But I'm still dead.
As for heroes—you were always mine.   Bookmark

my face in memory: Ennis Willliam shown here,
dead brown boy beneath a laughing white
bird   and a startling halo of question marks

Bill C., for atonement—erasure

For un-original sin

Our father.
          Thy name

   will be done
on earth.   It is in heaven.
Give   this   our daily bread
    for   s our debts,
as we forgive
          not   temptation
but   evil
for th   is   kingdom:
power and   glory for
  men.

The Stones of Giles Corey

The burdens of the world are cast as stones.
Some people grow a crop of rocks from seed,
carrot-baiting mules to haul their harvest.

You seem to balance boulders for, what—some test?
How strong am I, this back, these arms. More weight.
Well, that's been tried before—in Salem town.

At least Giles Corey bore crushing for principles,
defiant so his heirs could reap his lands.
What he could withstand, recumbent, silent
would have hard pressed any other man.

But we live in a locust-lousy world.
Once you fall broken, you lie stripped, when pride
has cored you, who will have gained at last
the field—the muleteer or the ass?

Ways and Means

After the Sacagawea golden dollar, minted since 2000

Bird Woman was *e pluribus unum*. An oddity—Sacagawea, Shoshone girl-guide. Token of peace amid men wending westward. Kidnapped, squawed at twelve. Bought, plural wife. By twenty-four, dead.

Beneath the Treaty Elm at Shackamaxon, the Turtle Clan (the Lenni Lenape) met William Penn. Both sides swore peace and amity. Wind took the tree, the pledges, their land. A plaque alone remains of the Delaware along the Delaware.

Today her golden coin is sold again. On the obverse "Liberty" crowns her placid gaze. *In God We Trust* blazons someone's faith. She smiles, perhaps forgiveness, half-breed son asleep against her shoulder, tribe emblems stamped out on Snake Squaw's back.

On the reverse a woman plants real riches: Three Sisters—squash, maize, beans. One symbol out of many. A peace pipe changes hands. Eagle soars. Turtle sticks out his neck. Turkey plumps for plucking. Wolf howls out a warning—too late.

A Representative from Delaware pled instead for Lady Liberty, Mother of Exiles, as the new American doubloon, our sovereign. One almighty golden dollar's worth. On her gilded back that weight—her trodden tribe, all those dead Presidents.

Gold Bum Rush

The Save Chinatown movement, Philadelphia

In Chinatown when hunting gold
the Suits rode through, careered, cajoled,
bulled round our reservations (in
the tradition of Americans),
and claimed our land. Soon dozers rolled,

choked our village in a stranglehold.
We summoned the warrior *chi* of old:
roused Lion and Dragon to battle again
in Chinatown.

What song the dirge bells might have tolled
without rapt resistance from the bold.
A warning by every citizen
of the people's right to self-determine—
not the stymied Suits we buffaloed
in Chinatown.

Cave Dwellers

In the Atacama Desert
the driest site on earth, nightly fog
moistens spiderwebs tiling the walls
of wind-cracked caves
where a hardy few extremophiles
like the microbe single-celled
green Dunaliella
cling to threads, adapt,
drink dew

In Philadelphia
some seventy percent of ex-cons
tangled in the web of urban streets
within three years of their release
reprise their single cell

Deserted
they thirst
they dangle
they cave
fall through

the crack

The Philadelphia Experiment: An Aesop's Fable

"...from electric fire thus obtained, spirits may be kindled..." — *Benjamin Franklin*

One spring day a boy chose to play hooky from school, skipping stones
in Wissahickon Creek. As he threw in bliss, a van slipped up. Three truant
officers slipped out: a priest, a sheriff, and Ben Franklin.

The priest armed himself with the Sign of the Cross, and exorcised the
errant boy with holy water. "Wretched knave, I shall pray till you convert
to learning." The Reverend bellowed a fiery homily till breathless. The boy
stared at him coolly. Meanwhile, from the van old Ben ransomed a kite.

The sheriff shoved the youth, knocking him over. "Punk, I'm locking you
in jail. No need to waste a desk," he railed. The boy glared at him, newly
aware of the rock his palm slid over.

Whistling, Franklin freed the kite. Aloft, bird-like, it skipped, milked the
blooming breeze. Under its fluttering silk a gold key bucked.

Wary, the boy drew up. "Yo, old man, what—"

"I'm going to catch lightning. You want some?" Franklin dared. Then
tendered him the kite string.

And the spark struck.

Moral: Tell the school officers to go fly a kite

The hitchhiking robot has been found dead

beheaded and dismembered in Philadelphia, where the lifeless life form was discovered in Olde City. The robot's followers were shocked and deeply saddened by the news.

A group calling itself "Nobots" has claimed responsibility. Their spokesperson, Dell E. Terious, issued this statement:

It's about jobs. It's about humanity.
We call on all Americans to oppose
the raw evil of automation.
We've struck a blow for human independence.
No bots! No bots! No bots!

They've released a video of the execution, where hooded members, holding raised machetes, chant:

Raw
evil demands
war
demands evil

Human rights activists have decried the killing. They've called the fringe crusaders savages, expressing outrage that the grinning guest—benign, child-sized, and helpless—was martyred in the cradle of liberty.

Still, the bot's creators have committed to continue their novel social experiment.

But Ms. Terious has cautioned more to come. Up next, a warning on the perils of hitchhiking.

This is Mark Jeering, Ferret News. And that's the way it is.

Donna Sleeps

1965-1974

Someone had to stay with the sleeping child
and I was awoken,
shaken from fitful sleep
by voices in the night,
the stillness broken.

Someone had to wait by the phone for news,
and I was the watcher.
This child at least is safe.
I checked his quiet slumber,
then thought of the other—

Picturing her laughing, dancing dark eyes,
the younger daughter;
the ivory skin,
the thick brown braids
—and the car that dragged her.

Someone had to choose when to turn them off,
the machines that breathed,
to harvest the organs,
what color the dress,
the verses to read.

Someone had to learn of a final sleep
from which no one awakens.
So much for promise,
innocence, and tomorrows
—all are taken.

I Knew a Man

for Gregory

I knew a man
    who could charm the coin from Charon's hand
    or Midas', too, squeeze lemonade from sand,
    hula rings like Saturn, drum thunder like Jupiter
    whenever he laughed, and he laughed some.

I knew a man
    who could dance on the head of a pin
    or the top of a bar. Around the pole he'd spin
    like a compass needle. His word—true north.
    He never called the shots—they begged to come.

This man, my friend,
    could thread a needle with a baseball bat,
    eclipse the sun, or wheedle cream from an alley cat.
    Always top dog, the black elephant in the room,
    he never took a back seat lest he throned it, Paul Bunyan-esque.

The man I knew
    could spin a yarn like Rumpelstiltskin
    or negotiate extra wishes from a jinn.
    His laser eyes could weep a secret out from a stone.
    He walked with Jesus upon the waters, two abreast.

Did you know my friend?
    He was the father of invention—and a muthuh, too.
    He switched the Grim Reaper gay, and broke the back of convention.
    He rose well-heeled, sprinkled motherwit like seed,
    his tongue, oil-slick. He could listen through the tips of his toes.

When Gabriel sounds
    that trumpet for the day of rest
    New Orleans-style, he'll strut at the head of the blessed,
    arm-in-arm with Peter and Michael, too.
    He'll be leading the band, prompting them their cue,
    this man I knew

Remembrance

Once my days have closed, you may not see
the road I travel. We are parted here
at last. I pray you will remember me,

not my seeming anger, impatiently
directed near you. That's how I hid my fear
once. My days have closed. You may not see

beneath the sternness, how it was to be
your father, to worry for the course you'd steer
at last. I prayed.... You will remember me

when you become a parent. Then you'll be
the sleepless one who worries through the years,
once my days have closed. You may not see

your strength yet. Now you're grown. All that debris
was your invention. Look—your way is clear
at last. I pray you will remember me,

and that you are my daughter. Finally,
seek love always. Don't be afraid to risk here.
Once my days have closed, you may not see
this last. I pray you will. Remember me.

To Charles Mason

On the 250ᵗʰ anniversary of the start of the Mason-Dixon survey, one of the original boundary stones was relocated to Charles Mason's cemetery and dedicated to him. His original grave location was unmarked, and is now unknown.

Christ Church Burial Ground,
Philadelphia
September 1, 2013.

Dear Sir,

I received your kind letter of September 27, 1786, and regretted to learn that plans for your latest astronomical project were sidelined by your unexpected demise. Such is the usual case. Be that as it may, since you have just become my next-door neighbor, and myself being presently very much at leisure, I shall endeavor to take up pen again to renew our correspondence, and offer my congratulations on the dedication of your new memorial headstone, one of the very same limestone mile markers you installed to outline your famously surveyed state boundary.

A regrettable business, to be sure, the misplacement of your original grave. Legacy is a tricky business. After one has quit the scene it is perhaps desirous to suppose that history might underline some contribution of merit, of durability, that some of one's words might get by-lined in some corner of the universe. Perhaps a school might bear one's name, a parkway, a museum, a bridge. Perhaps a statue. But one should not grow proud upon it. The Supreme takes amiss an excess of pomposity.

The Persian Empire headlined such monuments. *I am Cyrus, king of the world, great king...*Great capitals, like Philadelphia, at Pasargadae and Persepolis, filled with streamlined columned palaces whose bases were chiseled of magnificent white—and black—stones. Their Founding Fathers highly prized the strength of the stones over their color. They carved their history and their wisdom onto a clay barrel called the Cyrus Cylinder. Now only broken fragments gather dust. Like the lonely remnants of the Mason-Dixon Line. Perhaps posterity and time have ruled on the further need for your white line.

I confess I find Paradise a rather dull venue, having always been an active person. I prefer the bustle of a city—London, Paris, the incomparable Philadelphia, its pulsating lightning and skyscraping skyline, its modern minstrelsy and stellar history. Near the Schuylkill River, at 37th and Locust Streets, flourishes a grand old university where the doors of wisdom are never shut. Leave me a park bench with a newspaper or a good book. Find me there. We are now, are we not, quite at liberty.

    I remain your most obedient and humble servant,
B. Franklin.

Notes

A.M.E. African Methodist Episcopal Church. Founded in Philadelphia in 1816 by Richard Allen.

Rebecca Cox Jackson, Jarena Lee, Amanda Smith, and slave **Old Elizabeth** were 19th century black Philadelphia women who felt a calling to preach at a time when such influential roles were restricted to men.

"A.M.E.: III. Dr. Payne Has a Dream"

After South Carolina outlawed the education of Negroes on April 1, 1835, Payne was forced to close the school he had founded. He then moved to Philadelphia and became a leading figure in the early A.M.E. Church, historiographer and bishop for over forty years.

Wilberforce University (Ohio) was acquired by the A.M.E. in 1863. Payne became its president.

"Jarena's Appointment"

In 1819 Jarena Lee was the first woman to receive authorization to preach in the early A.M.E. Church but, as a female, could not be granted ordination. She became an itinerant minister.

"A.M.E.: II. Resistance"

"read us out of meeting" — expel from Methodist church membership

During church incorporation, the newly acquired Mother Bethel building was lost to the Methodist Episcopal Church through deliberate contract misrepresentation.

"Persecution by Three Ministers"

Facing strong opposition from A.M.E. Church ministers in her efforts to join their ranks, Rebecca Cox Jackson instead became an itinerant preacher. Later, as a Shaker Eldress, she founded an order of black Shakers in Philadelphia.

"Kings Yard, Old Calabar"

"high-toned" — upper-class (in fact or attitude), from a prominent family

Amanda Smith, of the Methodist Episcopal Church, also became an itinerant preacher, whose ministry included sojourns in Europe, India, and Africa.

"Eulogy" "published" — banned from preaching

"Torn" "rounds" — goes around.   "anatomy" — a skeleton.

"In Pandora's Box"

James Forten, an influential, wealthy black sailmaker, served as a seaman in the

Revolutionary War. When he was fifteen, his ship was captured by the British, and he became a prisoner of war.

Virginia slave Henry "Box" Brown obtained his freedom by hiding in a nailed-shut wooden box, which was then mailed to abolitionists in Philadelphia.

"Shadow Man"

"Monticello" — (Italian) little mount

Nearly one-fifth of the nation's population in the 1790 U.S. census were slaves. The Jeffersons' slave Sally Hemmings was also the half-sister of Jefferson's wife Martha.

"What Goes Around"

Oney Judge, a slave of President George Washington, escaped from his household while Philadelphia served as the nation's capital. She was never recaptured.

"The House on Third Street"

Richard Allen, his siblings, and their parents were slaves owned by the Honorable Benjamin Chew, together with a Philadelphia town house at 110 South Third Street. Chew sold the Allen family in 1768 to Delaware planter Stokeley Sturgis.

"Gift of Power" "rids" — removes

"Tanner's Blues"

Tanner's portrait of his mother (1897) was inspired by James McNeill Whistler's *Arrangement in Grey and Black No. 1, Portrait of the Artist's Mother* (1871), more commonly referred to as *Whistler's Mother.*

"Trans-plantation" *"ex situ"* — offsite

"Where William Walked"

Per the National Center for Education Statistics (2003), 22% of Philadelphia County lacks "basic prose literary skills."

"Mythopoesis: The Great Seal of the United States"

"shawbti" — servant statues that come alive to serve the deceased in the afterlife

In Philadelphia, on July 4, 1776, the Continental Congress appointed Benjamin Franklin, Thomas Jefferson, and John Adams as the first committee to design a Great Seal for the new country.

Like William Penn, President Richard M. Nixon was a Quaker. In the 1940s his parents owned a farm in Menges Mills, in York County, PA.

"Brother Marinus Dreams of North Korea"

From December 22-26, 1950 98,100 North Korean refugees and 105,000

U.N. and South Korean troops were evacuated from the besieged port city of Hungnam. Merchant Marine Capt. Leonard LaRue, a Philadelphia native, volunteered his ship, the SS *Meredith Victory*, to transport 14,000 of the refugees. This dangerous rescue, one of the largest sea evacuations in history, became known as the "Christmas Miracle."

Shortly after the Korean War ended, Capt. LaRue joined a Benedictine monastery in New Jersey, and became Brother Marinus.

"Bop: Major League"

"midnight" — In the early days of integration, referred denigratingly to an African-American

The Pythians was a black baseball club founded in Philadelphia by Octavius Catto and Jacob White, Jr. Catto, an educator and voting rights activist, was murdered on Election Day, 1871 at the age of 32.

On April 9, 1939 Marian Anderson's Easter Sunday concert at the Lincoln Memorial signaled a watershed moment in the struggle against "Jim Crow" segregation.

Song lyrics quoted in the poem were from Marian Anderson favorites "The Crucifixion" and "He's Got the Whole World in His Hands."

Octavius V. Catto, Marian Anderson, and Mo'ne Davis (from the Anderson Monarchs baseball team) all hail from South Philly. Davis is the first girl to score a win and pitch a shutout in Little League World Series history.

Catto and Anderson are both buried in historic Eden Cemetery, near Philadelphia.

"Bringing the Heat"

"mustard" — A high level of velocity on a pitch or throw

In August 2014, the Taney Dragons of Philadelphia finished third at the Little League World Series in Williamsport, PA. Their pitcher Mo'ne Davis became the first Little Leaguer featured on the cover of *Sports Illustrated*.

"Marian Fever"

The phrase "soaked myself in the music" is Marian Anderson's own, from her autobiography *My Lord, What a Morning*.

"That Summer, 1936"

Heavyweight boxer Joe Louis was nicknamed "The Brown Bomber."

"My Father's Art: Homage"

As a child in Philadelphia, Bill Cosby lived in the Richard Allen Homes, a low-income housing project. On January 16, 1997 Ennis William Cosby fell victim to a failed roadside robbery. He was 27.

Acknowledgements

To Willow Books and judge Remica Bingham-Risher, who honored this manuscript with the 2017 Willow Books Grand Prize for Poetry, to Marsh Hawk Press and judge Meena Alexander, who awarded the book the 2017 Robert Creeley Prize—sincerest gratitude. Thanks also to the Crab Orchard Series in Poetry First Book Award competition, that named it a semifinalist.

A sampling from this manuscript comprises "The Hitchhiking Robot Learns About Philadelphians," which won the 2016 Moonstone Chapbook Contest. Warm thanks to judge Afaa Michael Weaver and Larry Robin of Moonstone Press for this seminal opportunity.

With appreciation to the following contests for finalist designations: Salem College Rita Dove Poetry Award—"Shadow Man"; Atlanta Review International Poetry Competition—group "My Father's Art: Homage," "Mythopoesis: The Great Seal of the United States," "The Philadelphia Experiment: An Aesop's Fable," "To Charles Mason"; Farmingdale State College Paumanok Poetry Award—group "Bop: Major League," "Brother Marinus Dreams of North Korea, Christmas 1950," "Mythopoesis: The Great Seal of the United States," "My Father's Art: Homage." Also for semi-finalist placement: Naugatuck River Review Narrative Poetry Contest—"Bop: Major League"; Footnotes Charter Oak Award for Best Historical Poem— "My Man Richard."

Grateful thanks to the editors of the following publications where these works first appeared or are forthcoming:
823 on High: "Domestic"
African American Review: "Road Rules," "Bill C., for atonement—erasure"
Atlanta Review and Rosemont College anthology *Another Breath*: "Donna Sleeps"
Dear America: Reflections on Race anthology: "Firstborn"
Footnote: A Literary Journal of History and Moonstone Poetry Series's 2014 Anthology of Featured Poets: "My Man Richard"
Grayson Books anthology *Forgotten Women*: "Eulogy"
HIV Here & Now website (Indolent Books) for National Poetry Writing Month and World Aids Day: "I Knew a Man"
Mezzo Cammin: "Remembrance," "The Boat Banger"

Moonstone Poetry Series's 2016 Anthology of Featured Poets: "What Goes Around"
Naugatuck River Review: "Bop: Major League"
Referential: "Chris Botti's 'Cinema Paradiso'," "Pi Charting"
Whirlwind: "The Game," "Where William Walked"

To Marilyn Nelson: for the challenging tender of Rebecca Cox Jackson as a possible source of poetic inspiration to her 2009 New York City Cave Canem workshop—the launchpad that ignited this book—gratitude for banging this boat

Deep indebtedness to Rosemont colleague Ben Heins, Vasiliki Katsarou, and Kasey Jueds for their thoughtful critiques of portions of the manuscript; and to Eleanor Wilner, for her gracious and generous encouragement.

Always, for the bedrock: Mom, Phillip, Stephen, Elaine.

And to J.C. Todd, poetry godmother, for her singing scalpel.

Works Referenced

Adams, John. "1774. Thursday. Septr. 22." Founders Online. National Archives. http://founders.archives.gov/?q=%20third%20 street&s=1111311113&r=138.

Allen, Richard. *The Life, Experience, and Gospel Labours of the Rt. Rev. Richard Allen. To Which is Annexed the Rise and Progress of the African Methodist Episcopal Church in the United States of America. Containing a Narrative of the Yellow Fever in the Year of Our Lord 1793: With an Address to the People of Colour in the United States**. Philadelphia: Martin & Boden Printers, 1833.

Anderson, Marian. *My Lord, What a Morning.* New York: Viking Press, 1956.

Bradford, Sarah H. *Harriet: The Moses of Her People**. New York: Geo. R. Lockwood & Son, 1886.

Driskell, David C. *The Other Side of Color: African American Art in the Collection of Camille O. and William H. Cosby Jr.*. San Francisco: Pomegranate, 2001.

Du Bois, William Edward Burghardt and Isabel Eaton. *The Philadelphia Negro: A Social Study.* Philadelphia: Publications of the University of Pennsylvania, 1899. DuBoisopedia. "Du Bois, Burghardt." http://scua. library.umass.edu/duboisopedia/doku.php?id= about:du_bois_burghardt (photograph).

Elizabeth. *Memoir of Old Elizabeth, a Colored Woman**. Philadelphia: Collins, 1863.

Gilbert, Bill. *Ship of Miracles.* Chicago: Triumph Books, 2000.

Gillespie, Dizzy, with Al Fraser. *To Be, or Not...to Bop.* Minneapolis: University of Minnesota Press, 1979.

"Glossary of Baseball." Wikipedia. https://en.wikipedia.org/wiki/ Glossary_of_baseball.

Humez, Jean McMahon, ed. *Gifts of Power: The Writings of Rebecca Jackson, Black Visionary, Shaker Eldress.* Amherst, MA: The University of Massachusetts Press, 1981.

Jefferson, Thomas. *Notes on the State of Virginia*. Electronic Text Center, University of Virginia Library.

Lee, Jarena. *Religious Experience and Journal of Jarena Lee: Giving an Account of Her Call to Preach the Gospel*. Philadelphia: 1849.

Mathews, Marsha M. *Henry Ossawa Tanner: American Artist*. Chicago: University of Chicago Press: 1995.

McClure, Jim. "Richard Nixon's 1960 visit to York, No.3: It was a homecoming of sorts." York Town Square. Feb. 9, 2009. http://www. yorkblog.com/yorktownsquare/2009/02/09/nixon-no-3.

Nash, Gary B. "New Light on Richard Allen: The Early Years of Freedom." *The William and Mary Quarterly*. Third Series, Vol. 46, No. 2 (April 1989): 332-340.

Payne, Daniel Alexander. *History of the African Methodist Episcopal Church**. Edited by Charles Spencer Smith. Nashville, TN: Publishing House of the A. M. E. Sunday School Union, 1891.

————. *Recollections of Seventy Years**. Edited by Charles Spencer Smith. Nashville, TN: Publishing House of the A. M. E. Sunday School Union, 1888.

Runaway advertisement. *The Pennsylvania Gazette* (Philadelphia). May 24, 1796.

Robeson, Paul. *The Undiscovered Paul Robeson: An Artist's Journey, 1898-1939*. http://media.wiley.com/product_data/excerpt/59/04712426/0471242659. pdf (photograph).

Smith, Amanda. *An Autobiography: The Story of the Lord's Dealings with Mrs. Amanda Smith, the Colored Evangelist: Containing an Account of Her Life Work of Faith, and Her Travels in America, England, Ireland, Scotland, India, and Africa as an Independent Missionary**. Chicago: Meyer & Brother Publishers, 1893.
Smith, C.S. *A Monograph: The Life of Daniel Alexander Payne, D.D., LL.D*. Nashville, TN: Publishing House A.M.E. Church Sunday School Union, 1894.

Smith, W.O. *Sideman: The Long Gig of W.O. Smith*. Nashville, TN: Rutledge Hill Press, 1991."State & County Estimates of Low Literacy." National

Center for Education Statistics. Institute of Education Sciences. http://nces.
ed.gov/NAAL/estimates/ StateEstimates.aspx.

Still, William. *The Underground Railroad.* Project Gutenberg, 2005. http://www.
gutenberg.org/files/15263/15263-h/15263-h.htm.

Summers, Anthony. *The Arrogance of Power: The Secret World of Richard Nixon.*
New York: Viking, 2000.

Tighe, Samantha. "Philadelphia Comic Con 2013 Takes Over the Convention
Center." *The Temple News.* June 5, 2013. http://temple-news.com/
arts/2013/06/05/excelsior-comic-con-2013-takes-over-the-convention-center
(accessed July 21, 2013).

Washington, George. "Diary Entry: 22 September 1774." Founders
Online. National Archives. http://founders.archives.gov/?q=%20third%20
street&s=1111311113&r=139.

Weigley, Russell F., Ed. *Philadelphia: A 300-Year History.* New York: W.W. Norton
& Company, 1982.

The Lady from Philadelphia: Through Asia with Marian Anderson. VHS. Produced by
Dante J. James. Washington, D.C.: Kultur, WETA, 1991.

Williams, Richard E. *Called and Chosen: The Story of Mother Rebecca Jackson and
the Philadelphia Shakers.* ATLA Monograph Series, No. 17. Edited by Cheryl
Dorschner. Metuchen, N.J. & London: The Scarecrow Press, Inc. & The
American Theological Library Association, 1981.

Winch, Julie. *A Gentleman of Color: The Life of James Forten.* New York: Oxford
University Press, 2002.

"Witness: The Art of Jerry Pinkney" (painting *The Old African*). Philadelphia
Museum of Art exhibition (June 28, 2013-September 22, 2013). http://www.
philamuseum.org/exhibitions/787.html.

About the Author

Vernita Hall's *Where William Walked* was a 2017 Robert Creeley Prize winner and "The Hitchhiking Robot Learns About Philadelphians" won the 2016 Moonstone Chapbook Contest. Hall placed second in *American Literary Review*'s Creative Nonfiction Contest, and second runner-up for the *Los Angeles Review* Nonfiction Award. Poetry and essays appear or are forthcoming in numerous journals, including *Atlanta Review, Philadelphia Stories, Referential, Mezzo Cammin, Canary, African American Review*, and anthologies *Forgotten Women* (Grayson Books), *Not Our President* (Third World Press), *Dear America: Reflections on Race* (Geeky Press), *Boundaries and Borders* (Women of Color), and *Collateral Damage* (Pirene's Fountain). A LaSalle University alumna, Hall holds an MFA in Creative Writing from Rosemont College and serves on the poetry review board of Philadelphia Stories.